Quilt a New Christmas

WITH PIECE O'CAKE DESIGNS

Appliquéd Quilts, Embellished Stockings & Perky Partridges for Your Tree

Becky Goldsmith & Linda Jenkins

D1529518

C&T PUBLISHING

Text and artwork copyright © 2011 by Becky Goldsmith and Linda Jenkins

Photography and artwork copyright © 2011 by C&T Publishing, Inc.

Publisher: Amy Marson

Creative Director: Gailen Runge

Acquisitions Editor: Susanne Woods

Editor: Lynn Koolish

Technical Editor: Carolyn Aune

Copyeditor/Proofreader: Wordfirm Inc.

Cover Designer: Kristy Zacharias

Book Designer: Christina D. Jarumay

Production Coordinator: Zinnia Heinzmann

Production Editor: Julia Cianci

Illustrators: Becky Goldsmith and Zinnia Heinzmann

Photography by Christina Carty-Francis and Diane Pedersen of C&T Publishing, Inc., unless otherwise noted

Published by C&T Publishing, Inc., P.O. Box 1456, Lafayette, CA 94549

Library of Congress Cataloging-in-Publication Data

Goldsmith, Becky Marie, 1956-

Quilt a New Christmas with Piece O' Cake Designs : Appliquéd Quilts, Embellished Stockings & Perky Partridges For Your Tree / Becky Goldsmith and Linda Jenkins.

pages cm

ISBN 978-1-60705-177-0 (soft cover)

1. Christmas decorations. 2. Machine appliqué--Patterns. 3. Machine quilting--Patterns. I. Jenkins, Linda Jean, 1943- II. Piece O'Cake Designs. III. Title.

TT900.C4G65 2010

745.594'12--dc22

2010046182

Printed in China

10 9 8 7 6 5 4 3 2 1

Acknowledgments

We have all been there. That terrible moment when you realize that you have run out of a key fabric. When that happens to us, we can usually substitute something else. But Becky ran out of a crucial fabric in the border of *Circular Momentum,* and she could not find anything else that worked.

Christopher DeVoe from Baum Textile Mills came to the rescue. He was able to locate one yard of that green and white dot fabric for her. Thank you, Christopher and Baum Textiles!

Michelle Coker works in the Piece O' Cake office, which is in Linda's home in her sewing room. Michelle has become a great asset and blessing to Linda. While Linda was making the quilts for this book, Michelle handled much of the day-to-day Piece O' Cake business. She was (and still is) always eager to help in any way she can. Many times during the process, Linda would say, "Now what was I doing next?" Michelle would reply, "You need to stitch." Thanks, Michelle!

Dedication

From Linda

I dedicate this book to the creativity in all of us. I am often asked where I keep getting my ideas. My answer is: everywhere! I started with a basic idea for this book—Christmas. It is amazing where you find ideas that meld into other ideas.

I saw a picture of a room decorated for Christmas. It was not decorated in the usual traditional Christmas colors. The room had Christmas trees in lime green, hot pink, and blue. The tree skirt was orange tissue paper. Wow! What fun it would be to make a tree and village quilt using those colors, I thought. The colors and designs in this book were inspired by that one picture.

We are currently working on designing a collection of fabrics. While we were in Hawaii hiking in the rain forest, we saw so many plants that gave us ideas. Even lava rock created a great pattern. So take a hike, sip a cup of tea with a magazine, open your eyes. There is so much to see! Start your next quilt from the creative ideas flowing around you.

From Becky

Okay, I admit it. Linda was ready to work on a new Christmas book well before I was. She dragged me, practically kicking and screaming, into this book. I'm so glad she did because it has been fun!

Being in a partnership is a little bit like being married. It is important to accept the fact that you are not always going to think alike. You have to be able to happily live with the truth that you are not always going to be right. If you are going to succeed in a partnership, you have to learn how to communicate effectively—especially when you and your partner are not in agreement.

We have survived with both our friendship and partnership intact because Linda taught me how to be a good partner. In fact, what I have learned from Linda over the years has probably been good for my marriage. I sincerely appreciate it all.
Thank you, Linda!

Contents

Introduction

Christmas means so much to so many people. It is about family, faith, and hope for the future, and it is a celebration of where we are now. No wonder we quilters make so many Christmas quilts.

We make Christmas quilts with love in our hearts, to share that love with family and friends. We hope that you enjoy making—and sharing—many of the projects in this book.

Basic Supplies

Fabric The most common quilting fabric is 100% cotton. It is readily available, affordable, and easy to sew. *Always prewash your cotton fabric.*

Rotary cutter and mat For most cutting, including cutting strips, trimming blocks to size, and cutting borders, rotary cutting tools give you the best results.

Fabric scissors Small, sharp scissors are best for trimming fabric, clipping inner points, and clipping threads. Shears are best for cutting long seams.

Paper scissors Small, sharp scissors are more precise than long shears for cutting templates.

Clear upholstery vinyl To make the positioning overlay, use 54″-wide, clear, medium-weight upholstery vinyl from a store that carries upholstery fabric, or 18″-wide clear vinyl such as Quilter's Vinyl. Keep any tissue paper that comes with it.

Permanent markers To make the positioning overlay, a black Sharpie Ultra Fine Point Permanent Marker works best.

Thread Use cotton thread with cotton fabric.

Appliqué thread There are many brands to choose from. Work with different brands until you find the ones that work best for you. We prefer a finer cotton thread; these work well: Superior's MasterPiece, Aurifil 50-weight thread, Mettler 60-weight machine embroidery thread, DMC 50-weight machine embroidery thread, and YLI Soft Touch thread.

> ✿ **TIP**
>
> We have worked with Superior Threads to put together sets of MasterPiece thread called Frostings. The thread is pre-wound onto bobbins especially for appliquérs. The 36 different colors come in 3 sets of 12. Each bobbin holds 85 yards of thread. Small, compact, and convenient—these bobbin sets are a great way to carry your thread.

Piecing thread An all-purpose cotton thread like those made by Gütermann and Mettler works well for piecing. If you prefer a finer cotton thread, use one of our appliqué thread choices. When piecing with a finer thread, shorten your stitch length.

Machine quilting thread When we want the thread itself to be less obvious, we use the threads we recommend for hand appliqué (listed above) for our machine quilting. When we want a higher-profile thread, we use a heavier cotton thread like King Tut by Superior. We quilt heavily, so the finer thread is structurally sound. If you plan to quilt farther apart, you should use a heavier thread.

Hand quilting thread We like Gütermann's hand quilting thread.

Perle cotton hand quilting thread We like Prescencia's size 12 or 16 paired with a size 9 crewel embroidery needle.

Sewing machine For *piecing* you need a sewing machine in good working order that sews a straight stitch. Successful *machine quilting* requires the best sewing machine that you can afford. In both cases it's really helpful to have a table that your machine fits into.

Needles Use the appropriate needle for the job at hand.

Hand appliqué needles For hand appliqué, we use a size 11 Hemming & Son milliners needle. If you prefer a shorter needle, Clover's Gold Eye size 12 is nice. There are many good needles. Find the one that fits *your* hand.

Appliqué pins Use ½″ sequin pins to pin the appliqué pieces in place. Use larger flower-head quilting pins to hold the positioning overlay in place where necessary.

Pencils We are now using either Bohin or Sewline mechanical pencils. Choose white or gray, whichever shows up best on your fabric.

Clear heavyweight self-laminating sheets Use these sheets to make templates (pages 54–55). You can find them at most office supply stores, online, and sometimes at warehouse markets. Buy the single-sided sheets, not the pouches. If you can't find the laminate, use clear Con-Tact paper—it'll work in a pinch.

Sandpaper board When tracing templates onto fabric, place the fabric right side up on the sandpaper side of the sandpaper board. The boards are available in quilt shops, or make your own by gluing very fine-grit sandpaper to a thin piece of Masonite or plywood.

Wooden toothpick Use a round toothpick to help turn under the turn-under allowance at points and curves. Wood has a texture that grabs and holds the fabric.

Fusible web If you prefer to fuse and machine stitch the appliqué, use a paper-backed fusible web. Choose the one you like best, and follow the directions on the package. It's a good idea to test the fusible web on the fabric you will be using.

Shape-Flex All-Purpose Woven Fusible Interfacing Use fusible interfacing to add stability to the Christmas stocking fronts (page 38). Choose this brand (see Sources, page 63) or the fusible interfacing that you like best, and follow the directions on the package.

Nonstick pressing sheet If you are doing fusible appliqué, a nonstick pressing sheet will protect the iron and ironing board.

Batting We prefer to use a bamboo/cotton blend or a 100% cotton batting.

A good light Sewing is so much easier when you can see what you are doing. A floor lamp is particularly nice, as you can position it over your shoulder.

Quilting gloves Gloves make it easier to hold on to the quilt during machine quilting. We like the Machingers brand.

That Purple Thang Use this for turning the Perky Partridges (page 43) inside out.

Crushed walnut shells Otherwise known as Lizard Litter, this is a great product for stuffing pincushions. It is available at many pet stores.

Polyester stuffing This is used for the Perky Partridge Christmas ornaments (page 43).

Embellishments Add flair with rickrack, ribbon, floss, beads, and sequins.

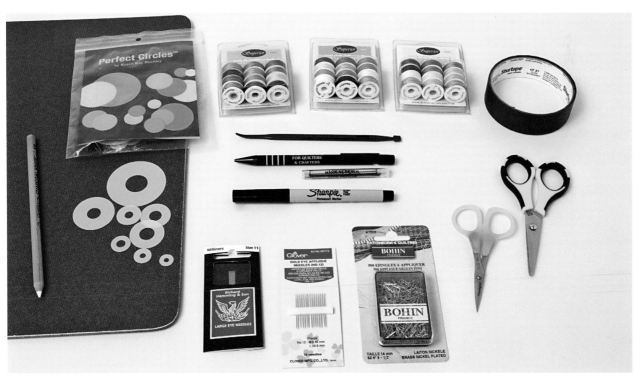

Sewing supplies

Color and Design

WHAT COLOR IS "CHRISTMAS"?

Red and green are *the* traditional Christmas colors. Interestingly enough, this is true no matter where you live. In fact, red and green are so linked to Christmas that it's hard to see them together and *not* think of Christmas.

Red and green are complementary colors, opposite each other on the color wheel. Complementary colors play together well. They are often graphic and full of energy. It is hard to mess up a combination of complementary colors. *If you are nervous about combining colors, this is important information!*

If red and green are the traditional Christmas colors, does that mean that everything Christmas *has* to be red and green? Thankfully, no, it does not. During the Christmas season, almost any color combination can *feel like* Christmas. Context is everything.

When the *design* itself says "Christmas," you have a lot more freedom in your color choices. Look at the colors Linda used in *Christmas in the Park* (page 16) to see what we mean. The blue, purple, pink, and orange trees practically sing with the joy of Christmas!

Have some fun, and color your Christmas projects with a rainbow of festive colors!

Christmas in the Park detail (full quilt on page 16)

CONTRAST AND VALUE

Before you pull every bright and happy fabric out of your stash, remember that the contrast between values is at least as important as color is in your quilt.

Every color has a value. It will be light, medium, dark, or somewhere in between. Contrast is the difference between two or more values. *It is the contrast between different values that makes a design visible.* Fabrics high in contrast that are placed next to each other are very visible. Fabrics low in contrast next to each other blend together.

Look at the green fabrics below. Yes, they are different shades of green and, yes, the prints are different from each other—but they are all medium value.

Even though these fabrics are different, they are so similar in color and value that it is hard to see the differences between them.

Because these fabrics are so similar in both color and value that you can't tell them apart, cutting them up and then sewing them back together into a quilt is a waste of your time if you want people to actually see the pattern.

When these fabrics are sewn together into four-patches, you can't see the pattern because there is no contrast between the values.

Adding light and dark values to the original stack of greens gives you something to work with. Now you can see the four-patch pattern because of the contrast in values.

Contrast between light, medium, and dark values makes the four-patch pattern visible.

Placing fabrics with high contrast next to each other in your quilt is one sure way of making that part of the design stand out. If you want to subdue an area, use fabrics of lower contrast. Most successful quilts have areas of both high and low contrast.

You may not be aware, but **just because two fabrics are different colors, they are not necessarily different values**. The blue and green below are different colors, but they look nearly the same. If you use them next to each other in a quilt, you won't be able to distinguish blue pieces from green pieces. That can ruin a design.

Fabrics that are different colors, but of similar value, can also run together and make patterns less visible.

Remember also that value is relative. A light yellow may be visible against a dark yellow, but the darkest yellow will still look very light against black. Always group together the fabrics that you plan to use in a particular quilt to evaluate which are light, medium, and dark.

DESIGNS ON FABRIC

Fabric comes in solid colors—and everything else.

Solid colors are just that, solid color. It's easy to think of solids as boring, but that's not true. Amish quilts, made only with solid fabrics, are wonderfully graphic. Many of today's art quilters use solids much as they would paint to create amazing quilts.

The "everything else" category is pretty crowded. Some prints are so subtle they almost look like solids. Others, composed of colors high in contrast, are very active. A printed fabric can have any design imaginable on it: tiny little dots, huge flowers, stripes, even Christmas trees!

Scale refers to the size of the design on the fabric. Large-scale designs look different from small-scale designs.

Small-, medium-, and large-scale prints

Some fabrics are quiet. Solids, tone-on-tones, and low-contrast prints tend to be quiet. Your appliqué will usually be easy to see on a quiet background.

Other fabrics are loud and busy. Busy fabrics tend to be prints that are composed of colors that are high in contrast. Big, busy prints can be fun and exciting when used as backgrounds behind your appliqué. Remember, however, that small appliqué pieces can get lost on a busy background.

Quiet versus loud

In the project instructions, we ask you to put all your appliqué on the backgrounds on your design wall before you begin sewing. This is the best time to evaluate how the appliqué fabrics are working on the backgrounds. If something isn't right, it's a lot easier to switch to something else before you've sewn it down.

CHOOSING FABRIC FOR A QUILT

Before we begin a quilt, the first thing we do is figure out what colors we want to work with—what is making us happy right then. We make a stack of fabric for each new quilt. In that stack are fabric choices for the backgrounds and for the appliqué. We don't worry about where we will use each fabric; that comes later. We just focus on fabric that we think might belong in the quilt we are about to make. We begin the stack with fabric from our stashes, adding new fabric from the quilt store as necessary.

When starting your quilt, *you* have to decide what *you* want to use. In some ways this is like deciding what clothes you want to put on in the morning. It's not necessary to overthink it. Monochromatic (one color) color schemes are simpler to work with than very colorful, scrappy color schemes. Quilts made from two values (light and dark) are simpler than more complex mixes of values. Look at the quilts in this book, and use them as a place to begin thinking about the colors you want to use.

After you have decided on colors and selected fabric, separate the background fabric from the appliqué fabric. If you have several background fabrics, stack them from darkest to lightest. This is not as hard as it sounds. Look at the fabric in front of you, and choose the darkest piece. Start the stack with this piece. Continue choosing the darkest fabric, placing it on the stack. You may or may not be able to use all of these fabrics.

Next, sort the appliqué fabrics by color. You might have a green stack, a red stack, a blue stack, and so on. Sort each color from dark to light as described above. Some fabrics could go in more than one stack. Does this orange belong in the red group or not? You can merge color stacks, blending from one color into another.

You are probably wondering why you are sorting and stacking your fabric, aren't you? What we have found is that it's easier to work from an organized group of fabric than it is to work from a disorganized pile. The more you arrange and rearrange the fabric in your stack, the more color combinations you will discover. Plus, it's fun to play with your fabric.

Place the stacks next to each other. Does the background work with the appliqué fabric? Do you have the necessary light, medium, and dark values to make your quilt? Are the colors working together? Any fabric that doesn't look good in the stack won't look any better cut up and sewn into your quilt. This is the time to remove any fabric that doesn't work. If a fabric isn't working, force yourself to put it away.

If you have trouble evaluating the fabrics in your stack, stand back and squint, or look at them through a reducing glass. Or better yet, take a digital picture of them. Sometimes you see more in a photo than you do when you're looking at the real thing. Know that this is a process that does get easier with practice.

When you are happy with the fabric you have chosen, cut and place the backgrounds up on the design wall. Begin adding the appliqué fabric in whatever order makes sense to you.

Place all the setting blocks, sashing, and borders—all the parts of the quilt—up on the wall. Take a giant step back and really look at your work. Squint, use a reducing glass, take a picture—do whatever it is you need to do to help yourself evaluate your quilt. Begin stitching the appliqué only when you are happy with all of your fabric choices.

Fabric stacks

Projects

Christmas in the Park

Made by Linda Jenkins,
quilted by Mary Covey

Finished quilt: 45˝ × 61˝

Pull out your shiniest beads and flashiest trim, and enjoy embellishing this park full of Christmas trees and the festive houses that surround them.

MATERIALS

- **Light center backgrounds:** 1½ yards

- **Red border backgrounds:** 1 yard

- **Pieced vertical strips in the center background:** A variety of fabrics to total ½ yard

- **Red and white dot inner border:** ¼ yard

- **Red and white dot side border:** ¼ yard

- **Green side border:** ⅜ yard

- **Red dot fabric for scallops:** ½ yard

- **Appliqué:** A variety of large scraps

- **Binding:** 1 yard

- **Backing and sleeve:** 4⅛ yards

- **Batting:** 53″ × 69″

Additional supplies:

- **Clear upholstery vinyl for positioning overlays:** 1¼ yards (54″ wide) or 3¾ yards (18″ wide)

- **Self-laminating sheets for templates (clear, single-sided, heavyweight; 9″ × 12″):** 14 sheets

- **Sharpie Ultra Fine Point marker**

CUTTING

- **Light center backgrounds**

  A: Cut 1 strip 21¼″ × 46″ (from the lengthwise grain) for the larger background.

  B: Cut 1 strip 9¼″ × 46″ (from the lengthwise grain) for the smaller background.

- **Red border backgrounds**

  Cut 3 strips 10″ × 40″ for the top and bottom borders, seam them together end to end as needed, and cut into 2 strips 10″ × 47″ for the top and bottom borders.

- **Pieced vertical strip in the center block**

  Cut 20 strips 2½″ × 8½″ for the pieced vertical strip in the background.

  Cut 2 strips 3¼″ × 8½″ for the top and bottom strips of the pieced vertical strip in the background.

- **Red and white dot inner border fabric**

  Cut 3 strips 1″ × 40″ for the side inner borders, seam them together end to end as needed, and cut into 2 strips 1″ × 44½″ for the side inner borders.

  Cut 2 strips 1″ × 37½″ for the top and bottom inner borders.

- **Red and white dot side border fabric**

  Cut 5 strips 1″ × 40″, seam them together end to end as needed, and cut into 4 strips 1″ × 45½″ for the side borders.

- **Green side border fabric**

  Cut 7 strips 1½″ × 40″, seam them together end to end as needed, and cut into 6 strips 1½″ × 45½″ for the side borders.

- **Cut fabric for appliqué needed.**

- **Binding**

  Cut 1 square 26″ × 26″ to make a 2½″-wide continuous bias strip 240″ long. (See Making Continuous Bias Strips, page 50.)

CENTER ASSEMBLY

Refer to General Appliqué Instructions (pages 53–60). Appliqué patterns are on pullout pages P1–P4.

1. Make templates for the center appliqués (Trees #1–9 and #11). Refer to the quilt assembly diagram (page 20) for the tree sizes needed.

2. To make a pattern for the background, cut or construct a piece of paper 36″ × 44″. This is the finished size of the center. Draw horizontal and vertical center lines on the paper. Make a copy of each tree pattern. Trim the excess paper away from the trees. Place and tape the trees in position on the background paper. Refer to the photo of the quilt (page 16) and/or the quilt assembly diagram (page 20) for placement.

Use the side and corner scallop patterns to trace the scallops onto your pattern. Note that the side scallop is different from the corner scallop. Place the patterns on your background pattern, lining up the dashed lines on the scallops with the line at the edge of your background pattern. The side scallops touch but don't overlap. The corner scallops overlap the side scallops.

Make your overlay from this pattern; include the center lines.

3. Sew the 2½″ × 8½″ strips together to make the pieced vertical strip. Sew a 3¼″ × 8½″ strip to each end of the pieced vertical strip. Press the seam allowances toward the bottom of the quilt.

4. Sew the light background A to the left side of the pieced strip. Press the seam allowances toward A.

5. Sew the light background B to the right side of the pieced strip. Press the seam allowances toward B.

6. Your background should measure 38″ × 46″. Draw a line ¾″ in from the outer edge on each edge of your background. Press the block background in half horizontally. Place it on your design wall.

7. Place the overlay over the background. It will be helpful to draw a line on the overlay, marking each of the long vertical pieced seamlines. Be careful not to mark on the background!

❖ AUDITION THE ENTIRE QUILT

Read ahead in these instructions. It's a good idea to get all of your borders (with the border appliqué pieces) on your design wall *before* you begin any stitching.

8. Cut out the appliqué pieces, adding ³⁄₁₆″ turn-under seam allowances on all edges (see Step 9 before cutting out the scallops). Place the appliqué pieces onto the background on your design wall. Use the overlay to get them in the proper position, or place them by eye. Play with your color/fabric choices until you are happy with the way your quilt looks.

9. The templates for the scallops and corner scallops are a little different. The dashed lines indicate the seamlines at the edges of the quilt center. The straight edges of the scallops are sewn into the pieced edge of the quilt. The straight edge of each scallop template includes the ¼″ seam allowance. Trace around these templates. When you cut the fabric shapes, add the ³⁄₁₆″ turn-under allowance on the curved side of each scallop as you do with all needle-turn appliqué pieces. The straight edges, which already include the ¼″ pieced seam allowance, are cut directly on the drawn line.

The overlay is big. If you want to, you can cut it in half lengthwise. Make a cut between the vertical center and the left vertical piecing lines. Use the pressed-in center lines and/or the piecing lines to line up the side of the overlay you are using.

10. Appliqué the scallops first: Line up the straight cut edge of the scallops with your overlay *and* with the line you drew on your background. The drawn line helps to keep the scallops straight.

11. Use the cutaway appliqué technique (pages 61–62) on small or narrow pieces, windows, and doors as you appliqué each block.

12. Add any soft embellishments as you appliqué or when your appliqué is complete. Hard embellishments are added through all the layers, after your quilt is quilted.

13. When your appliqué is complete, press the quilt center on the wrong side, and trim it to 36½″ × 44½″.

 TIP

Decorate your houses and trees with rickrack or other cute soft embellishments after the appliqué is complete. Sew on hard embellishments such as sequins and beads after quilting. Sew through all layers of the quilt when adding hard embellishments.

APPLIQUÉ BORDER ASSEMBLY

Refer to General Appliqué Instructions (pages 53–60). Appliqué patterns are on pullout pages P1–P4.

1. Cut or construct a piece of paper 8″ × 45″. Make copies of Houses #12–15; Trees #2–6, #8, and #10; and the snowman for each border. Refer to the assembly diagram (page 20) for the tree sizes needed. Trim away the excess paper from the copies, and place the appliqué patterns in position. Tape them in place, and make your overlay from this pattern.

2. Make templates for the top and bottom borders.

3. Press the top and bottom border backgrounds in half horizontally and vertically. Place them on your design wall.

4. Cut out the appliqué pieces, adding ³⁄₁₆″ turn-under seam allowances on all edges, and place them on the wall. Play with the placement until you are happy with the way your quilt looks.

5. Appliqué the borders. Add any soft embellishments as you appliqué or when your appliqué is complete.

6. When your appliqué is complete, press each border on the wrong side. Trim the borders to 8½″ × 45½″.

PIECED SIDE BORDER ASSEMBLY

Sew 2 red and white dot border strips together with 3 green border strips to make a side border. Press toward the darker strips. Repeat to make the other side border.

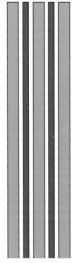

Pieced border assembly diagram

QUILT ASSEMBLY

Refer to the quilt assembly diagram (page 20) for quilt construction.

1. Sew an inner border strip to each side of the quilt. Press toward the inner border.

2. Sew an inner border strip to the top and bottom of the quilt. Press toward the inner border.

3. Sew the pieced side borders to the quilt. Press the seam allowances toward the borders.

4. Sew the top and bottom appliqué borders to the quilt. Press the seam allowances toward the borders.

5. Layer and baste the quilt. Quilt by hand or machine.

6. Stitch any hard embellishments to your quilt.

7. Finish the quilt (pages 49–52).

Quilt assembly diagram

QUILT A NEW CHRISTMAS WITH PIECE O' CAKE DESIGNS

The All Wonderful Red & Green Quilt

Made by Linda Jenkins,
quilted by Mary Covey

Finished quilt: 61″ × 61″

 Linda tweaked the traditional Christmas colors of red and green in this quilt. The green background is unexpected—and fresh! The red and white prints sparkle.

Listed below are the templates that Linda used on each fabric. Several of those templates are used on more than one fabric. To match Linda's quilt, refer to the quilt photo before you trace your appliqué shapes.

- **Light green block and border backgrounds:** 4¼ yards

- **White with large red dots (#1 in blocks):** ¼ yard

- **Red with large white dots (#2–5 in blocks, #1–4 in borders, #1–5 in border corners):** 1¼ yards

- **Red with small white dots (#5 in blocks, #1–4 in borders, #1–5 in border corners):** ⅔ yard

- **White with small red dots (#6 in blocks):** ¼ yard

- **White with very small red dots (#7 in blocks):** ⅓ yard

- **White with teeny red dots (#7 in blocks):** ⅜ yard

- **Red tone-on-tone stripe (#5, #8 in blocks; #5, #16 in borders; #6 in border corners):** 1½ yards

- **Red with small white dots (#7, #9, #11, #18, #20, #22 in borders; #8, #10, #12 in border corners):** ¼ yard

- **White with medium red dots (#6, #8, #10, #17, #19, #21 in borders; #7, #9, #11 in border corners; and sashing):** 1¼ yards

- **A variety of red and white dots or prints (remaining #5 petals):** ⅔ yard

- **Binding:** ⅞ yard

- **Backing and sleeve:** 4¼ yards

- **Batting:** 69″ × 69″

Additional supplies:

- **Clear upholstery vinyl for positioning overlays:** 1 yard (54″ wide) or 2 yards (18″ wide)

- **Self-laminating sheets for templates (clear, single-sided, heavyweight; 9″ × 12″):** 4 sheets

- **Sharpie Ultra Fine Point marker**

CUTTING

- **Green border and block backgrounds**

  Cut 4 strips 9″ × 49″ for the border backgrounds (from the lengthwise grain).

  Cut 9 squares 17″ × 17″ for the block backgrounds.

  Cut 4 squares 9″ × 9″ for the border corners.

- **White with medium red dot sashing**

  Cut 3 strips 1″ × 40″, and cut them into 6 strips 1″ × 15½″ for sashing strips A.

  Cut 8 strips 1″ × 40″, seam them together end to end as needed, and cut into 4 strips 1″ × 46½″ for sashing strips B and 2 strips 1″ × 47½″ for sashing strips C.

- **Cut fabric for appliqué as needed.**

- **Binding**

  Cut 1 square 29″ × 29″ to make a 2½″-wide continuous bias strip 280″ long. (See Making Continuous Bias Strips, page 50.)

BLOCK ASSEMBLY

Refer to General Appliqué Instructions (pages 53–60). Appliqué patterns are on pullout pages P3–P4.

1. Make templates and overlays for the appliqué.

2. Press the block backgrounds in half horizontally and vertically. Place them on your design wall.

3. Cut out the appliqué pieces with their turn-under allowances. Place the appliqué pieces on the backgrounds on your design wall. Play with your color/fabric choices until you are happy with the way your quilt looks.

❖ AUDITION THE ENTIRE QUILT

Read ahead in these instructions. It's a good idea to get all of your borders (with the border appliqué pieces) on your design wall before you begin any stitching.

4. Use the cutaway appliqué technique (pages 61–62) on small or narrow pieces as you appliqué each block.

5. When your appliqué is complete, press the blocks on the wrong side. Trim the blocks to 15½″ × 15½″.

APPLIQUÉ BORDER ASSEMBLY

Refer to General Appliqué Instructions (pages 53–60). Appliqué patterns are on page 25 and pullout pages P3–P4.

1. Make templates and overlays for the borders and border corners.

2. The border pattern is repeated 3 times in each border. Press the border backgrounds in half horizontally and vertically. Press an additional vertical crease 15″ to the right and to the left of the center on each border strip. These creases correspond to the dashed center lines on the border pattern.

3. Press the border corner backgrounds in half horizontally and vertically.

4. Place the border and corner backgrounds on your design wall around the blocks.

5. Cut out the appliqué pieces, and place them on the wall. Play with their placement until you are happy with the way your quilt looks.

6. Appliqué the borders and border corners.

7. When your appliqué is complete, press each border and border corner on the wrong side. Trim the borders to 7½″ × 47½″. Trim the border corners to 7½″ × 7½″.

QUILT ASSEMBLY

Refer to the quilt assembly diagram (page 24) for quilt construction.

1. Sew a sashing strip A between the blocks in each row. Press toward the sashing strips.

2. Sew a sashing strip B between the rows and to the top and bottom of the quilt center. Press toward the sashing strips.

3. Sew a sashing strip C to each side of the quilt. Press toward the sashing strips.

4. Sew the side borders to the quilt. Press the seam allowances toward the borders.

5. Sew a border corner to each end of the top and bottom borders. Press toward the border strips. Sew the top and bottom borders to the quilt. Press the seam allowances toward the borders.

6. Layer and baste the quilt. Quilt by hand or machine.

7. Finish the quilt (pages 49–52).

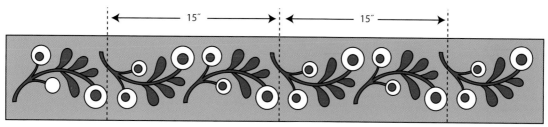

←—— 15″ ——→ ←—— 15″ ——→

Center placement overlay on each vertical crease.

Quilt assembly diagram

QUILT A NEW CHRISTMAS WITH PIECE O' CAKE DESIGNS

The All Wonderful Red & Green Quilt Border Corner Pattern

Caribbean Christmas

Made and quilted by Linda Jenkins

Finished quilt: 28½˝ × 48˝

Cute and quick to make, this happy combination of birds and flowers will add a festive sparkle to your home.

MATERIALS

- **Pink vertical backgrounds:** 1½ yards

- **Pieced vertical strips in the background:** A variety of fabrics to total ½ yard

- **Narrow red side border:** ¼ yard

- **Wide light side border:** ½ yard

- **Appliqué:** A variety of large scraps

- **Binding:** ⅔ yard

- **Backing and sleeve:** 1⅞ yards

- **Batting:** 37″ × 56″

Additional supplies:

- **Clear upholstery vinyl for positioning overlays:** 1 yard (54″ wide) or 1½ yards (18″ wide)

- **Self-laminating sheets for templates (clear, single-sided, heavyweight; 9″ × 12″):** 4 sheets

- **Sharpie Ultra Fine Point marker**

CUTTING

- **Pink vertical backgrounds**

   Cut 2 strips 8″ × 50″ (from the lengthwise grain).

- **Pieced vertical strip in the background**

   Cut 22 strips 2½″ × 7″ for the pieced vertical strip in the background.

   Cut 2 strips 3¼″ × 7″ for the top and bottom strips of the pieced vertical strip in the background.

- **Narrow red side border fabric**

   Cut 5 strips 1″ × 40″, seam them together end to end as needed, and cut the new strip into 4 strips 1″ × 48½″ for the side borders.

- **Wide light side border fabric**

   Cut 8 strips 1½″ × 40″, seam them together end to end as needed, and cut into 6 strips 1½″ × 48½″ for the side borders.

- **Cut fabric for appliqué as needed.**

- **Binding**

   Cut 1 square 22″ × 22″ to make a 2½″-wide continuous bias strip 180″ long. (See Making Continuous Bias Strips, page 50.)

CENTER ASSEMBLY

Refer to General Appliqué Instructions (pages 53–60). Appliqué patterns are pages 28–29 and pullout page P3.

1. To make a pattern for the background, cut or construct a piece of paper 20½″ × 48″. Draw horizontal and vertical center lines on the paper. Make 3 copies of the bird pattern and 3 mirror-image copies of the bird pattern. Make 3 copies of the border section and 6 copies of the daisy. Trim away the excess paper from around the copies; then place and tape the designs in position on the background paper pattern. Refer to the photo of the quilt (page 26) and/or the quilt assembly diagram (page 28) for placement. Make your overlay from this pattern.

2. Make the appliqué templates.

3. Sew the 2½″ × 7″ strips together to make the pieced vertical strip. Sew a 3¼″ × 7″ strip to each end of the pieced vertical strip. Press the seam allowances toward the bottom of the quilt.

4. Sew a light background to each side of the pieced strip. Press the seam allowances toward the sides.

5. Press the background in half horizontally and vertically. Place it on your design wall.

6. Cut out the appliqué pieces with their turn-under allowances. Place the appliqué pieces on the background on your design wall. Use the overlay to get them in the proper position, or place them by eye. Play with your color/fabric choices until you are happy with the way your quilt looks.

✤ AUDITION THE ENTIRE QUILT

Read ahead in these instructions. It's a good idea to get your entire quilt on the design wall before you begin any stitching.

7. Use the cutaway appliqué technique (pages 61–62) on small or narrow pieces as you appliqué the quilt.

8. When your appliqué is complete, press the quilt on the wrong side. Trim the center to 21˝ × 48½˝.

PIECED BORDER ASSEMBLY

Sew 3 light border strips together with 2 red border strips to make a side border. Press toward the red strips. Repeat to make the other side border.

QUILT ASSEMBLY

Refer to the quilt assembly diagram (at right) for quilt construction.

1. Sew the side borders to the quilt. Press the seam allowances toward the borders.

2. Layer and baste the quilt. Quilt by hand or machine.

3. Finish the quilt (pages 49–52).

Quilt assembly diagram

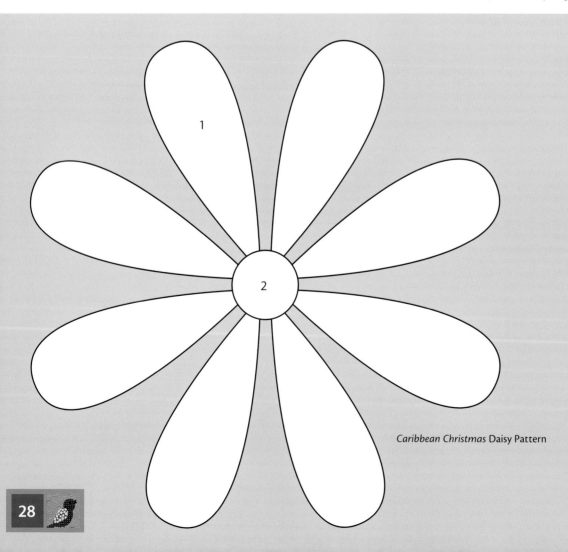

Caribbean Christmas Daisy Pattern

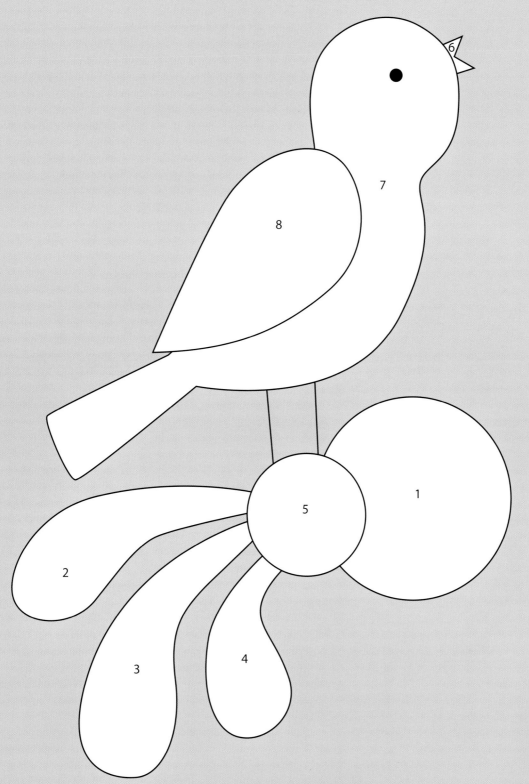

Caribbean Christmas and *Christmas Stocking* Bird Pattern

Circular Momentum

Made and quilted
by Becky Goldsmith

Finished quilt: 77″ × 77″

 The energy found in circles is beautifully captured in this delightfully spinning design.

MATERIALS

Listed below are the yardage amounts with the corresponding template numbers that Becky used.

- **Light block and border backgrounds:** 6 yards
- **Green block corners:** ¾ yard
- **Purple flowers:** 1¼ yards
- **Blue spokes (#1 and #1–3 in the border corner blocks):** ½ yard
- **Purple flowers (#2 and #8 in the borders):** 1¼ yards
- **Blue and green print (#3, #9, and #9 in the borders):** ⅓ yard
- **Light green stripe (#4):** ⅛ yard
- **Light green (#5):** ¼ yard
- **Green and blue plaid (#6):** ¼ yard
- **Turquoise blue (#7):** ⅓ yard
- **Dark turquoise blue (#8):** ⅜ yard
- **Green print (#1–2 in the borders):** ⅜ yard
- **Green print (#3–4 in the borders):** 1 yard
- **Green print (#5–7 in the borders):** ⅞ yard
- **Turquoise blue inner border:** ⅓ yard
- **Binding:** 1 yard
- **Backing and sleeve:** 5¼ yards
- **Batting:** 85″ × 85″

Additional supplies:

- **Clear upholstery vinyl for positioning overlays:** 2 yards (54″ wide) or 4 yards (18″ wide)
- **Self-laminating sheets for templates (clear, single-sided, heavyweight; 9″ × 12″):** 3 sheets
- **Sharpie Ultra Fine Point marker**

CUTTING

- **Light block and border backgrounds**

  Cut 4 strips 10″ × 63″ (from the lengthwise grain) for the border backgrounds.

  Cut 4 squares 32″ × 32″ for the block backgrounds.

  Cut 4 squares 10″ × 10″ for the border corner backgrounds.

- **Green block corners**

  Cut 8 squares 8⅞″ × 8⅞″.

- **Turquoise inner border fabric**

  Cut 8 strips 1″ × 40″, seam them together end to end as needed, and cut into 2 strips 1″ × 60½″ for the side inner borders and 2 strips 1″ × 61½″ for the top and bottom inner borders.

- **Binding**

  Cut 1 square 33″ × 33″ to make a 2½″-wide continuous bias strip 340″ long. (See Making Continuous Bias Strips, page 50.)

BLOCK ASSEMBLY

Refer to General Appliqué Instructions (pages 53–60). Appliqué patterns are on pullout page P2.

1. Make the templates and overlay for the block.

2. Press the block background in half horizontally and vertically. Place it on your design wall.

3. Cut out the appliqué pieces with their turn-under allowances. Place the appliqué pieces on the background on your design wall. Play with your color/fabric choices until you are happy with the way your quilt looks.

♣ AUDITION THE ENTIRE QUILT

Read ahead in these instructions. It's a good idea to get all of your borders (with the border appliqué pieces) on your design wall before you begin any stitching.

4. Appliqué the blocks. Use the cutaway appliqué technique (pages 61–62) for the long narrow strips. Use the circle appliqué technique (page 62) for the circles. Remember, circles take a little more time to appliqué well. Don't rush, and your circles will be prettier.

5. When your appliqué is complete, press the blocks on the wrong side. Trim the blocks to 30½″ × 30½″.

6. The block corners must be trimmed on the diagonal. It is low-tech, but the best way to do this accurately is to draw an 8⅛″ × 8⅛″ square on a piece of paper. Cut it in half diagonally. Make the triangle into a template, using clear laminate. Place this template on each corner of each block, and trim along the long diagonal line.

7. Cut the 8 green 8⅞″ × 8⅞″ squares in half on the diagonal. Sew a triangle to each corner of each block. Press the seam allowances toward the block.

BORDER ASSEMBLY

Refer to General Appliqué Instructions (pages 53–60). Appliqué patterns are on pullout page P4).

1. One-half of the border pattern is provided. Make your overlay from this pattern. Be sure to include (and label) the lines indicating the center and end of the border, as well as the appliqué shapes that extend past the center line. Flip the overlay upside down to position appliqué pieces on the other end of each border.

2. Make an overlay for the border corners.

3. Make templates for the borders and border corners.

4. Press the border and border corner backgrounds in half horizontally and vertically. Place them on your design wall.

5. Cut out and place the appliqué pieces on the wall. Play with the color placement until you are happy with the way your quilt looks.

6. Appliqué the borders. The #7 circles at the ends of each border strip overlap the border corners. You will appliqué them after the quilt has been sewn together.

Do not sew the flowers to the borders or border corners until the quilt has been sewn together.

7. When your appliqué is complete, press each border on the wrong side. Trim the borders to 8½″ × 61½″. Trim the border corners to 8½″ × 8½″.

QUILT ASSEMBLY

Refer to the quilt assembly diagram (page 33) for quilt construction.

1. Sew the blocks together into rows. Press in alternate directions.

2. Sew the rows together. Press toward the bottom.

3. Make a placement overlay of just the flower at the center of the quilt. Include the center lines. Position this placement overlay over the center of the quilt where the 4 blocks meet. Place and then appliqué the flower, being careful not to stretch the edges of the blocks.

4. Sew an inner border to each side of the quilt. Press toward the inner border.

5. Sew an inner border to the top and bottom of the quilt. Press toward the inner border.

6. Sew a border to each side of the quilt. Press toward the inner border.

7. Sew a border corner to each end of the 2 remaining borders. Press the seam allowances toward the border corners.

8. Sew the top and bottom borders to the quilt. Press the seam allowances toward the inner borders.

9. Appliqué the #7 circles at the corners of the borders.

10. Position the flower placement overlay at the center and corners of each border. Refer to the border patterns for placement. Position and appliqué each flower.

11. Layer and baste the quilt. Quilt by hand or machine.

12. Finish the quilt (pages 49–52).

Quilt assembly diagram

A Treat before Takeoff!

Designed by Linda Jenkins,
hand and machine appliquéd
by Linda Jenkins and Lori Gray,
machine quilted by Mary Covey

Finished quilt: 37″ × 42″

 This quilt is a treat for the eyes
during the Christmas season,
and everybody likes a treat—
even Rudolph!

MATERIALS

- **Blue print for top background:** ½ yard

- **Light prints for center background:** ⅔ yard each of 6 fabrics OR ⅔ yard of 1 fabric

- **Snow in center:** ⅓ yard

- **Blue prints for bottom background:** ⅜ yard of 2 fabrics OR ½ yard of 1 fabric

- **Green inner border:** ¼ yard

- **Blue and green dot borders:** ½ yard

- **Appliqué fabrics:** A variety of small to large scraps; Linda used wool for the snowman and his scarf and Santa's beard and mustache.

- **Binding:** ¾ yard

- **Backing and sleeve:** 3 yards

- **Batting:** 45″ × 50″

Additional supplies:

- **Clear vinyl for positioning overlays:** 1 yard (54″ wide) OR 2 yards (18″ wide)

- **Self-laminating sheets for templates (clear, single-sided, heavyweight; 9″ × 12″):** 11 sheets

- **Sharpie Ultra Fine Point marker**

- **Narrow red rickrack for "Merry Christmas":** 4 yards

- **Quilter's Choice Basting Glue**

- **Black #8 perle cotton for the reindeer's antlers, tail, mouth, and eyes**

- **Brown-black embroidery floss for the snowman's arms**

- **Embroidery floss for the carrot tops and Santa's bootlaces**

- **Buttons, beads, and trims for embellishment**

CUTTING

- **Top background**

  Cut 1 strip 12″ × 32″.

- **Center background**

  Cut 2 strips 6¼″ × 19″, one for each end of the background, and 4 strips 5½″ × 19″, for the center of the background OR

  Cut 1 strip 19″ × 32″.

- **Snow in center**

  Cut 1 strip 10″ × 32″.

- **Bottom background**

  Cut 2 strips 6¼″ × 10″, one for each end of the background, and 4 strips 5½″ × 10″, for the center of the background OR

  Cut 1 strip 10″ × 32″.

- **Inner border fabrics**

  Cut 2 strips 1″ × 35½″ for the side inner borders.

  Cut 2 strips 1″ × 31½″ for the top and bottom inner borders.

- **Border fabrics**

  Cut 2 strips 3½″ × 36½″ for the side borders.

  Cut 2 strips 3½″ × 37½″ for the top and bottom borders.

- **Cut fabric for appliqué as needed.**

- **Binding**

  Cut 1 square 26″ × 26″ to make a 2½″-wide continuous bias strip 200″ long. (See Making Continuous Bias Strips, page 50.)

CENTER ASSEMBLY

Refer to General Appliqué Instructions (pages 53–60). Appliqué patterns are on page 37 and pullout pages P1–P4.

1. Make templates for all 3 sections. You will also need copies to make the paper patterns as described in Steps 2–4, below.

2. To make a pattern for the top section, cut or construct a piece of paper 10″ × 30″. Draw a horizontal and vertical center line on the paper. Make 1 copy each of Houses #13, #14, and #15 and 1 copy each of Small Tree #5, Small Tree #4, and Tree #8. Trim the excess paper away from the houses and trees. Place and tape the copies in position on your paper background pattern. Refer to the photo of the quilt (page 34) and/or the quilt assembly diagram (page 37) for placement.

3. To make a pattern for the center section, cut or construct a piece of paper 17″ × 30″. Draw a horizontal and vertical center line on the background paper. Draw a line marking the top of the snow on your background pattern. There is no right or wrong place to put your snow—just draw a line. Make 1 copy of Santa and Rudolph. Trim away the excess paper; place and tape the copies in position on your background pattern. Match the vertical and horizontal lines on the copy to the center dashed lines on your pattern.

❖ THE SNOW

You can make a large template for the snow, OR you can trace the snow line directly onto the strip of snow fabric.

4. To make a pattern for the bottom section, cut or construct a piece of paper 8″ × 30″. Draw a horizontal and vertical center line on the paper. Make a copy of the words "Merry Christmas" and of the snowman. Feel free to substitute "Merry Christmas" written in your own handwriting. Trim away the excess paper, and place and tape the copy in position on your background pattern. Refer to the photo of the quilt and/or the quilt assembly diagram for placement.

5. Tape the 3 patterns together. Make a copy of Tree #1. Trim away the excess paper, and place and tape the tree in position over the taped-together patterns. Separate the 3 sections, cutting Tree #1 apart where the sections meet, leaving a paper pattern for each section.

6. Make your overlays from the 3 paper patterns.

7. If piecing the center background, sew the 5 ½″-wide pieces together side by side, and add a 6¼″-wide piece to each end. Press the seam allowances to one side. Repeat for the bottom background.

8. Press each background in half horizontally and vertically. Place them on your design wall.

9. Cut out the appliqué pieces with their seam allowances. Place the appliqué pieces on the backgrounds on your design wall. Use the overlays to get them in the proper position, or place them by eye. Play with your color/fabric choices until you are happy with the way your quilt looks.

10. Appliqué each section. Tree #1 will be appliquéd after the 3 background pieces have been sewn together. (See Quilt Assembly, Step 2, below.) Use the cutaway appliqué technique (pages 61–62) on small or narrow pieces. Add rickrack and/or embroidery to each block as indicated.

❖ WRITING "MERRY CHRISTMAS"

Linda used Quilter's Choice Basting Glue to hold the narrow rickrack in place. The glue is water soluble, and the instructions say it washes out completely. She then couched the rickrack down with red thread.

11. When the appliqué is complete (except for Tree #1), press the quilt top on the wrong side.

12. Trim the top portion to 10½″ × 30½″.

13. Trim the center portion to 17½″ × 30½″.

14. Trim the bottom portion to 8½″ × 30½″.

QUILT ASSEMBLY

Refer to the quilt assembly diagram (page 37) for quilt construction.

1. Sew the 3 background pieces together. Press the seam allowances toward the bottom of the quilt.

2. Appliqué Tree #1 to the quilt, leaving the area that falls over the side border unsewn.

3. Sew the side inner borders to the quilt. Press the seam allowances toward the inner borders.

4. Sew the top and bottom inner borders to the quilt. Press the seam allowances toward the inner borders.

5. Sew the side borders to the quilt. Press the seam allowances toward the borders.

6. Sew the top and bottom borders to the quilt. Press the seam allowances toward the borders.

7. Finish appliquéing Tree #1.

8. Layer and baste the quilt. Quilt by hand or machine.

9. Finish the quilt (pages 49–52).

10. Add embellishments. For extra stability, stitch hard or heavy items through all 3 layers of the quilt.

Quilt assembly diagram

A Treat before Takeoff! Snowman Pattern

The Stockings Were Hung by the Chimney with Care...

Made by Becky Goldsmith

Finished stocking: 12″ × 21″

 The Christmas stocking pattern (on pullout page P2) is a good size for decorating your mantel and for filling with presents. You can use the pattern as it is drawn, or you can use it as a guide, varying the shape of each stocking.

MATERIALS

- **Stocking front:** 1 or more fabrics to total ½ yard

- **Stocking back:** ½ yard

- **Optional stocking cuff:** ¼ yard

- **Stocking lining:** ⅔ yard

- **Appliqué:** A variety of small to large scraps

- **Optional wool for names:** ⅛ yard

Additional supplies:

- **Clear upholstery vinyl for positioning overlays if necessary for your design:** ⅓ yard

- **Self-laminating sheets for templates (clear, single-sided, heavyweight; 9″ × 12″):** 3–4 sheets

- **Ribbon for hanging loop:** 6″ per stocking

- **Shape-Flex All-Purpose Woven Fusible Interfacing** (See Sources, page 63.)

- **Embellishments:** Buttons, beads, sequins, ribbon, paint—be creative!

❖ TOYS AS EMBELLISHMENTS!

Notice the tiny cars on Jack's stocking and the antique wood Scrabble tiles on Christopher's stocking. Small, colorful, and happy—toys make great embellishments. Becky drilled tiny holes in the Scrabble tiles and stitched them on with #8 perle cotton. The cars were stitched down with #8 perle cotton on their axles, behind the wheels.

 FROM BECKY

My Aunt Helen made wonderful Christmas stockings for my brother, sister, and me for our first Christmases. We have used them all our lives; mine is 55 years old—imagine that! When my boys were born, my mom made stockings for them. I made stockings for my daughters-in-law and my grandchildren.

When Lorna, Christopher's wife, was pulling out her Christmas decorations in 2009, she realized that their stockings were gone. Really gone. This was especially hard on Christopher, who had had his stocking for 27 years. But after a deep sigh, we let them go, and they made do with the promise of new stockings in 2010.

What you see here are their new stockings. I made each stocking to suit its owner. Lorna loves birds and the color green. Christopher, who is working on a PhD in English, chose just the right words for his stocking. Elanor, my granddaughter, is the personification of perky pink, and her little brother, Jack, is a truck guy.

This is a Christmas project that is fast and easy enough for a beginner. But better than that, this is a project that you can make for someone special, who may keep and use it for a lifetime!

STOCKING ASSEMBLY

Refer to General Appliqué Instructions (pages 53–60). Stocking pattern is on pullout page P2 and optional bird appliqué pattern is on page 29.

Note: The stocking pattern includes a ¼″ seam allowance.

1. Make a template from the stocking pattern. If you are going to place appliqué on your stocking, make templates for the appliqué pieces.

2. If you are piecing your stocking front, do so now. Refer to String-Pieced Stocking (page 41) or Pieced Checkerboard Stocking (page 42).

3. If you are going to add embellishments to the stocking front, stabilize it now with Shape-Flex fusible interfacing or a similar product.

4. Place 2 layers of the fabric, right sides together, on your cutting mat. Place the stocking back fabric right side down on the lining fabric and the stocking front fabric right side up on top of the stack.

5. Place the stocking template on top of the stack. Make sure the toe is pointing in the direction you want it to. Pin the stack if necessary to keep it from shifting. Trace around the stocking template onto the top fabric. Cut through all the layers of fabric on the drawn line with a rotary cutter or shears.

♣ CHANGING THE SHAPE OF THE STOCKING...

When making several stockings that will hang together, consider changing the shape of each one. Use the pattern as a guide, altering it to make the stocking bigger or smaller, wider or narrower. You can make these changes directly on the fabric, or you can make a new template for each new shape. If you turn the pattern over, you can make stockings that hang pointing in the opposite direction.

6. Appliqué and embellish the stocking front. If you are adding a cuff to your stocking, leave the top 3½″ free from embellishments. Wait until Step 13 to add the name to the cuff.

♣ ADDING NAMES...

Names can be written with ribbon, rickrack, sequins, paint, embroidery floss, or other similar materials. Names can be appliquéd using the cutaway appliqué technique. Becky drew the names for her stockings on wool and cut them out, being careful to keep the edges smooth. She sewed the wool letters down with perle cotton in a running stitch.

7. Sew the stocking front and back right sides together with a ¼″ seam, leaving the top of the stocking open. Clip the inner curves at the back of the heel and bottom of the foot, and turn. Press the seam so that it is smoothly curved and flat.

8. Sew the 2 linings right sides together. Trim the seam allowance to ⅛″.

9. If you are *not* adding a cuff, place the stocking, right side out, inside the lining. The stocking and the lining will be right sides together. Match the top raw edges of the lining and stocking, and pin them together.

Place stocking inside lining, matching raw edges. Pin lining and stocking together.

10. Sew the lining to the stocking, leaving a 3″ opening on the back side of the top of the stocking.

11. Pull the stocking out through the opening. Maneuver the lining inside the stocking.

Pull stocking out through opening.

12. Hand sew the opening closed, and go to Step 17 to finish the stocking.

13. If you are adding a cuff, measure across the top of the stocking, from seam to seam. This measurement may vary from stocking to stocking. To get the length of the cuff strip, multiply this number by 2, and add ½″ for the seam allowances. Cut your cuff strip 7½″ × the length you just calculated.

14. Fold the cuff strip wrong sides together lengthwise, and press to crease. Open the cuff strip, and sew the ends right sides together. Press the seam allowances open, and refold along the crease.

15. Place the lining, wrong side out, inside the stocking, which is right side out. Match the top raw edges of the lining and stocking. Place the folded cuff right side out inside the stocking. Place the seam of the cuff at the center back of the stocking. Match all the raw edges at the top of the stocking. Sew the cuff, lining, and stocking together with a ¼˝ seam.

16. Pull the cuff out from inside the stocking, and fold it over the top raw edges. Add the name to the cuff.

Fold cuff over to cover seam.

17. Cut a 6˝ piece of ribbon or trim to make a loop. Sew the loop to the stocking at the top inside corner.

PIECED STOCKING FRONTS

String-Pieced Stocking

1. Cut a light solid base fabric that is big enough for your stocking.

2. Cut several strips of fabric in a variety of widths × 14˝ long.

3. Place your first strip right side up at one end of the base fabric. Place the second strip right side down on it at the bottom of the first strip, matching the raw edges. Sew through all 3 fabrics using a ¼˝ seam allowance.

4. Fold the strip over the seam so that both strips are right side up. Press the seam. Place the next strip right side down at the bottom of the most recent strip. If you want to place it at an angle, that's fine. Sew the strip with a ¼˝ seam allowance. If you placed the strip at an angle, carefully trim away excess strip fabric that extends past the ¼˝ seam.

Trim to ¼˝ seam allowance.

Add strips, changing the angle if you want to. Carefully trim away excess fabric as necessary.

5. Continue adding strips until the pieced unit is big enough for your stocking. To save fabric, follow the contour of the stocking shape.

❖ CRAZY-PIECED STOCKING

Elanor's crazy-pieced stocking was made using a variation of string piecing. Construct small pieced units. These units can be made from strips, squares, or triangles. This is a good place to use up leftover bits from other pieced projects.

Sew the units into ever bigger units until you have enough to make a stocking. You can work on a base fabric to add stability, or you can fuse the Shape-Flex woven fusible interfacing to the back of the piecing.

Pieced Checkerboard Stocking

- Cut 5 dark strips 2½″ × 20″.

- Cut 5 light strips 2½″ × 20″.

1. Sew a dark strip to a light strip. Press the seams toward the dark strip. Repeat for all the strips.

2. Cut each pair of strips into units 2½″ × 4½″.

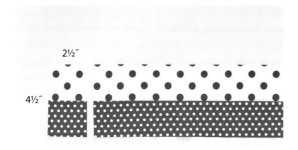

2½″

4½″

Cut each pair of strips into units 2½″ × 4½″.

3. Sew 3 pairs together into a row. Make 12 rows (more if you have changed your stocking design to be bigger than the pattern given). Press the seam allowances toward the dark fabric. Refer to the checkerboard assembly diagram, and sew the rows together. Press the seams in one direction.

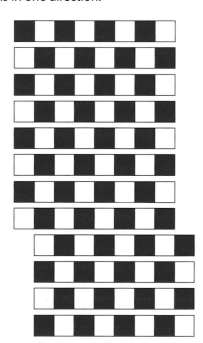

Checkerboard assembly diagram

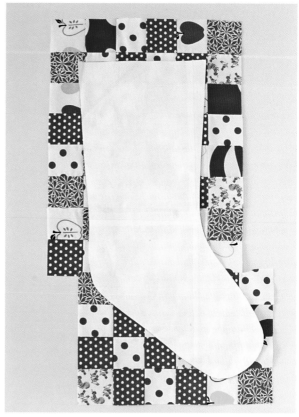

Follow contour of stocking shape when piecing your checkerboard.

4. Fuse Shape-Flex woven fusible interfacing to the back of the piecing to add stability if desired.

✤♣ OPPORTUNITY KNOCKS (FOR SPARE BLOCKS)!

Do you have leftover blocks or pieced units from quilts you have made in the past? Or perhaps you have some antique blocks. Go through that stash of blocks—you may be able to use them in a Christmas stocking!

Perky Partridge
Pincushion/Ornament

Made by Becky Goldsmith

 Use your prettiest fabric scraps and this simple pattern to make a whole flock of adorable birds. They look cute scattered around your house, and they make wonderful presents. Use the wide bird base to make pincushions, or use the narrow bird base template to make Partridge in a Christmas Tree ornaments.

MATERIALS

- **Bird body:** A fabric scrap

- **Bird base:** A fabric scrap

Additional supplies:

- **Self-laminating sheet for templates (clear, single-sided, heavyweight; 9″ × 12″): 1 sheet**

  - **That Purple Thang tool made by Little Foot**

  - **Sequins and seed beads for bird eyes**

  - **Crushed walnut shells for pincushion's filling OR polyester stuffing for ornament's filling**

  - **Decorative pins: Quilter's pins, Tacky Glue, and wool beads**

  - **Wooden clothespin, Elmer's glue, glitter, and hot glue for ornament**

PERKY PARTRIDGE ASSEMBLY

Refer to General Appliqué Instructions (pages 53–60). Patterns are on page 47.

Note: Pattern pieces include a ¼″ seam allowance.

1. Make the bird body and bird base templates. Use an awl, stiletto, or ice pick to poke small holes through the dots.

2. Place the bird body template right side up on the right side of the fabric for one side of the bird. Trace around the template onto the fabric. Place the bird body template right side up on the wrong side of the fabric for the other side of the bird. Trace around the template onto the fabric. Cut out both sides of the bird body on the drawn lines.

3. Place the bird base template right side up on the wrong side of the bird base fabric. Trace around it. Cut it out on the drawn line.

4. Mark through the holes in the templates to make small light dots on the wrong side of each body and base piece.

5. Place one bird body right sides together with the bird base. Match the dots at the beak end of the bird. Pin the bird base to the bird body, curving the base as necessary to match the raw edges.

6. Sew from dot to dot on the bird base piece, backstitching at each end.

Sew from dot to dot with bird base facing up.

7. Pin the other bird body to the open edge of the base of the bird unit, matching the dots at the beak end and raw edges as before. Sew from dot to dot, leaving a 1½″ opening in the center of the seam.

8. Move the seams at the base of the bird out of the way, and pin and then sew the remaining edges of the bird bodies together. Be sure to sew as close as you can to the intersection of the seams at the base of the bird so that stuffing cannot escape.

Leave open.

Move seams out of way, and sew bird bodies together.

9. Clip the inner points on each side of the bird beak. Trim away the dog-ear from the end of the bird beak. Trim the seam on each side of the beak to ⅛″.

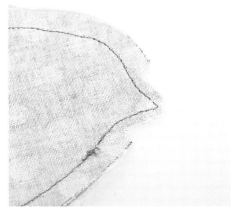

Clip inner points, trim seams to ⅛″, and trim dog-ear at end of beak.

10. Turn the bird right sides out through the opening on the bottom. Carefully push out the beak with That Purple Thang or a similar tool. Run the tool firmly inside the bird, along each seam, until the seams are smooth.

11. We like to stuff our **pincushions** with crushed walnut shells (also known as Lizard Litter). It's a little messy, so work over a plate or tray. Use a funnel to direct the crushed walnut shells into the pincushion. Stop every now and then and use your finger to pack the crushed shells firmly in place. Be sure to fill the beak and head. When you have filled the pincushion with as many crushed shells as you can, carefully stitch the opening closed.

12. Stuff **Christmas ornaments** with polyester stuffing. The birds will look much better if you pack the stuffing in firmly, but be careful not to make your stuffing lumpy. Read the tip at right before you stuff.

13. The birds are more festive with topknots, and these are easy to make. Choose a quilter's pin with a round head in a color that works with your bird. Place a generous dab of Tacky Glue on the shaft of the pin where it meets the pinhead. The glue can extend onto the head of the pin.

14. Stick the pin through the hole in a wool bead. Slide the bead up the pin until the head of the pin is just inside the wool bead. If you think you need more glue, slide the bead down, add more glue, and slide the bead back in place. Stick it in the pincushion, and let it dry. Be creative! You can use all sorts of beads on all sorts of pins and make decorative pins for all your pincushions!

Glue wool bead to pin, add more glue

15. Sew a sequin and seed bead to each side of the bird's head for eyes.

♣ HEAD AND TAIL FEATHERS FOR CHRISTMAS ORNAMENTS

To keep the head and tail feathers in place on your Christmas ornaments, coat the first ¼″ of the pin with Tacky Glue before sticking it into the bird. Or, for something a bit more secure, cut 3 lengths of a suitably heavy bendable wire 8″, and twist them together at the center. Open the seam at the top of the head and at the tail. Place the wires inside the bird, poking the ends through the holes in the seam. Stuff the bird, keeping the wires in the middle of the bird. Tack the seams shut around the wires. Trim the wires to the right length, and glue wool beads to the end of each one.

16. To make the clothespin base for your Christmas ornament, squirt some Elmer's glue onto a disposable plastic plate. Add a little bit of water to thin the glue. Using a small disposable brush, coat a wooden clothespin with glue. While the glue is still wet, sprinkle it liberally with glitter. Let it dry.

17. Use hot glue to attach your bird to the glittery clothespin.

Glue glittery clothespin to bird.

QUILT A NEW CHRISTMAS WITH PIECE O' CAKE DESIGNS

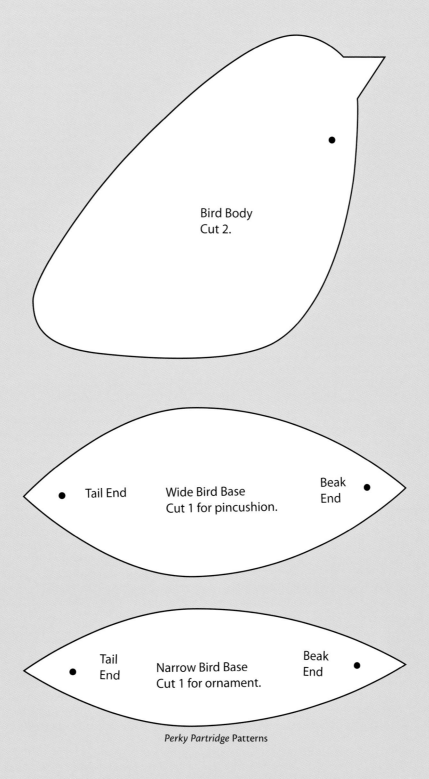

Bird Body
Cut 2.

Tail End   Wide Bird Base   Beak
              Cut 1 for pincushion.   End

Tail   Narrow Bird Base   Beak
End   Cut 1 for ornament.   End

Perky Partridge Patterns

General
Quiltmaking
Instructions

FABRIC PREPARATION

Prewash your fabric before using it. Prewashing is a good way to test for colorfastness and shrinkage. It is better that the fabric bleeds or shrinks before it is sewn into the quilt. Prewashed fabric has a better hand, and it smells better. In addition, washing removes the chemicals in the fabric that some people are allergic to. Prewashed fabric appliqués better because it frays less.

We wash cotton fabric in the washing machine using Orvus Paste. Orvus Paste is a neutral synthetic detergent that can be bought by the gallon. It is soluble in both hot and cold water and rinses out freely. It is intended to be used on animals large and small—and it is wonderful for cotton fabric! Use 1–2 tablespoons of Orvus Paste per washer load.

It's a good idea to have Synthrapol and Retayne on hand when washing fabric and quilts. Synthrapol is a product that you add to the wash water to keep dye molecules that come out of the fabric from depositing back into the fabric. Retayne helps keep the dye molecules in the fabric to begin with. Because water chemistry varies, it is important for you to experiment a little to find out how these products work best for you. You can also use the Color Catcher sheets made by Shout. Follow the manufacturer's instructions.

Dry cotton fabric in the dryer on warm. Do not add a dryer sheet, because it adds softness to the fabric that makes it a little harder to work with. Remove fabric from the dryer while it is still warm. Smooth out the wrinkles, and fold it to fit your shelf or drawer. It is not necessary to press fabric at this point. You will need to press it before you cut it.

 ABOUT OUR FABRIC REQUIREMENTS

Cotton fabric is usually 40″–44″ wide off the bolt. To be safe, we calculate all our fabric requirements based on a 40″ width.

Use the fabric requirements for each quilt as a guide, but remember that the yardage amounts vary depending on how many fabrics you use and the sizes of the pieces you cut. Our measurements allow for both fabric shrinkage and a few errors in cutting.

SEAM ALLOWANCES

All machine piecing is designed for ¼″ seam allowances.

FINISHING THE QUILT

1. Assemble the quilt top following the instructions for each project.

2. Construct the back of the quilt, piecing as needed.

3. Place the backing right side down on a firm surface. Tape it down to keep it from moving around while you baste.

4. Place the batting over the backing, and pat out any wrinkles.

5. Center the quilt top right side up over the batting.

6. Baste together the layers. Yes, we thread baste for both hand and machine quilting.

7. Quilt by machine or by hand.

8. Trim the outer edges, leaving ¼″–⅜″ of backing and batting extending beyond the edge of the quilt top. This extra fabric and batting will fill the binding nicely.

9. Finish the outer edges with continuous bias binding.

MAKING CONTINUOUS BIAS STRIPS

We use binding cut on the bias grain of the fabric because it wears better. Bias strips, or longer lengths of continuous bias, also make very good vines because they are flexible and curve gracefully.

For binding, we normally cut our strips 2½˝ wide. This strip is pressed in half lengthwise, wrong sides together. The raw edges are sewn even with the quilt top, and the folded edge is turned to the back and hand stitched over the raw edges of the quilt. (See Sewing Binding to the Quilt, pages 51–52.)

Bias from Strips

1. Cut several strips on the bias at the designated width. Angle both ends at the same 45° angle.

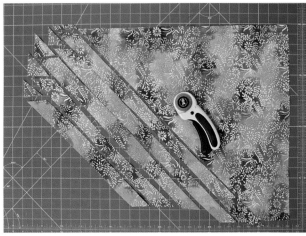

Cut strips on bias with angled ends.

2. Place 2 strips right sides together. Offset the ends so that a V is formed at the ¼˝ seamline.

3. Sew them together, end to end, with a ¼˝ seam. Press the seams open. Trim away the dog-ears that extend beyond the edges of the strips.

Place strips together with offsetting ends, and sew together.

4. Press the binding strip in half lengthwise, wrong sides together.

Bias from a Square

When you need a length of bias made from one fabric, the following method works very well. A surprisingly small amount of fabric makes quite a bit of bias, and there is no waste.

1. Start with a square of fabric, and cut it in half diagonally. Refer to the project instructions for the size of the square.

2. Sew together the 2 triangles with right sides facing, as shown. Be sure to sew the edges that are on the straight of grain. If you are using striped fabric, match the stripes. You may need to offset the fabric a little to make the stripes match.

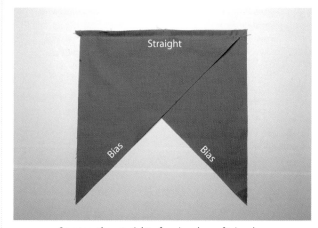

Sew together straight-of-grain edges of triangles.

3. Press the seam allowances open. Make a short cut 2½˝ wide into each side as shown. Cuts are always made on the bias grain of the fabric. Check the grain-line before you cut.

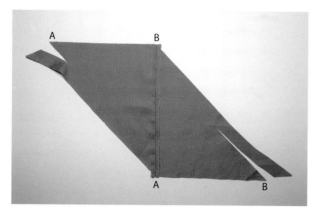

Make short cut 2½˝ wide.

4. Match the A's and B's with the fabric right sides together. Pin and sew. Press the seam open.

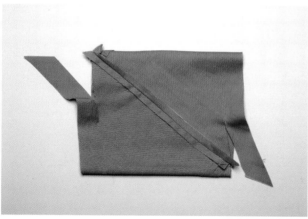

Pins, sew, and press.

5. Use a rotary cutter and ruler to cut the continuous bias strip 2½˝ wide.

6. Press together the length of bias strip wrong sides for double-fold binding.

SEWING THE BINDING TO THE QUILT

1. Be sure the outer edges of the quilt are trimmed (page 49).

2. Cut the first end of the binding at a 45° angle. Turn under this end ½˝, and press.

3. With raw edges even, pin the binding to the edge of the quilt top, beginning a few inches away from a corner. Start sewing 6˝ from the beginning of the binding strip, using a ¼˝ seam allowance and the walking foot.

4. Stop ¼˝ away from the quilt top's corner, and back-stitch several stitches.

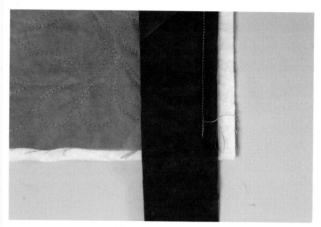

Stop ¼˝ from corner and backstitch.

5. Fold the binding straight up as shown. Note the 45° angle.

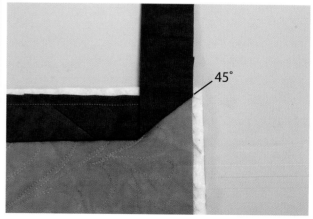

Fold binding up.

6. Fold the binding straight down, and begin sewing the next side of the quilt.

Fold down binding, and sew.

7. Sew the binding to all sides of the quilt, following the process in Steps 4–7. Stop a few inches before you reach the beginning of the binding, but don't trim the excess binding yet.

8. Overlap the ends of the binding, and cut the second end at a 90° angle. *Be sure to cut the binding long enough so the cut end is covered completely by the angled end.*

9. Turn under ¼", and finger-press the angled end. Slip the 90° end into the angled end.

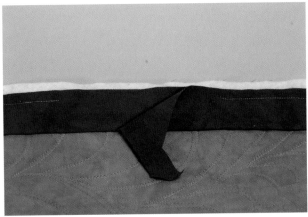

Slip 90° end into angled end.

10. Pin the joined ends to the quilt, and finish sewing the binding to the quilt.

Pin joined ends, and finish sewing.

11. Turn the binding to the back of the quilt, covering the raw edges. If there is too much batting, trim some to leave your binding nicely filled. Hand stitch the folded edge of the binding to the back of the quilt. Hand stitch the mitered corner edges down as well.

MAKING A LABEL AND SLEEVE

1. Make a hanging sleeve, and attach it to the back of the quilt.

2. Make a label, and sew it to the back of the quilt. Include information you want people to know about the quilt. Your name and address, the date, the fiber content of the quilt and batting, the special person or occasion the quilt was made for—these are all things that can go on the label.

SIGNING YOUR QUILT

We have come to the conclusion that it's a good idea to put your name on the front of your quilt as well as putting a label on the back. There are a variety of ways to do this:

▪ You can appliqué your initials and the date on the quilt top.
▪ You can add information with embroidery or a permanent pen.
▪ You can quilt your name and the date into your quilt with matching or contrasting thread.

General Appliqué Instructions

PREPARING THE BACKGROUNDS FOR APPLIQUÉ

Always cut the background fabric larger than the size it will be when it is pieced into the quilt. The outer edges of the block can stretch and fray as you handle it while stitching. The appliqué can shift during stitching and cause the block to shrink slightly. For these reasons it is best to add 1˝ to all sides of the backgrounds when you cut them out. We have included this amount in the cutting instructions for each quilt. You will trim the blocks to size after the appliqué is complete.

1. Cut the backgrounds as directed in the project instructions. For blocks with pieced backgrounds, cut and sew them together as directed.

2. Press each background block in half vertically and horizontally. This establishes a center grid in the background that will line up with the center grid on the positioning overlay. (Refer to page 57.)

3. Use a pencil to draw a ¼˝-long mark at the edge of the block on top of each pressed-in grid line. Be sure not to make the lines too long, or they will show on the block. These little lines will make it easier to correctly position the overlay as you work with it and will help you find the center when trimming your block.

4. Use a pencil to draw a little X in one corner of the block background. This X will be in the same corner as an X that you will draw on the overlay. Be sure to place the X near the edge so it won't show on the finished block.

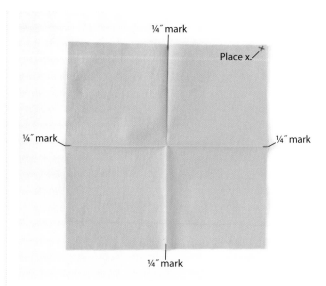

Draw ¼˝-long lines at each end of pressed-in grid and draw small X in one corner.

MAKING APPLIQUÉ TEMPLATES

Each appliqué shape requires a template, and we have a unique way to make templates that is both easy and accurate.

1. Use a photocopier to make 1–3 copies of each block. If the pattern needs to be enlarged or reduced, make these changes *before* making copies.

❖ DETERMINING THE NUMBER OF COPIES

You need a complete paper shape for each appliqué piece that requires a template. When one shape lies over another, you need 2 copies. Look at each shape to determine how many copies it requires—or make 3 copies of each pattern, knowing that you'll probably have some extra copies.

2. Cut out the appliqué shapes from these copies. Cut them in groups when you can—it saves on the laminate (page 9). Leave a little paper allowance around each shape or group. Where one shape overlaps another, cut the top shape from one copy and the bottom shape from another copy.

3. Place a self-laminating sheet shiny side down on the table. Peel off the paper backing, leaving the sticky side of the sheet facing up.

4. If you are doing **hand appliqué**, place the templates *drawn side down* on the self-laminating sheet. For **fusible appliqué**, place the *blank side down*. Take care when placing each template onto the laminate. Use more laminating sheets as necessary.

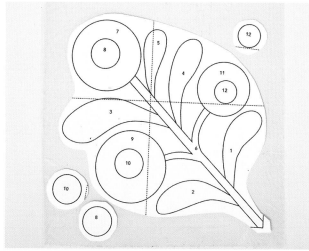

For hand appliqué, place appliqué shapes **drawn** side down on self-laminating sheets.

For fusible appliqué, place appliqué shapes **blank** side down on self-laminating sheets.

5. Cut out each shape. Try to split the drawn line with your scissors—don't cut inside or outside the line. Keep edges smooth and points sharp.

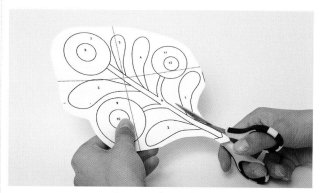

Cut out each template.

You'll notice how easy these templates are to cut out. That's the main reason we like this method. It is also true that a mechanical copy of the pattern is more accurate than hand tracing onto template plastic. As you use the templates, you will see that they are sturdy and hold up to repeated use.

USING THE TEMPLATES

The templates are numbered. The numbers indicate the stitching sequence. Begin with #1 and work your way through the block. The templates are used with the shiny laminate side up. **Hand appliqué** templates are placed with the drawn, shiny side up on the right side of the fabric. **Fusible appliqué** templates are placed on the wrong side of the fabric with the blank, shiny side up.

✳ *note*

*We have reservations about recommending the use of fusible web. We aren't sure how the chemicals in it will affect the fabric over time. However, if you choose to use fusible web, follow the manufacturer's instructions. Use a nonstick pressing cloth to protect the iron and ironing board from the fusible web. Be sure to test the fabrics you plan to use. Iron the fusible web to the **wrong** side of the appliqué fabric. Do not peel off the paper backing until later.*

1. For **hand appliqué**, place the appliqué fabric right side up on a sand-paper board (page 9). For **fusible appliqué,** place the fabric with the wrong side up. (The fusible web side will be up.)

2. Place the template right side up (shiny laminate side up) on the fabric with as many edges as possible on the diagonal grain of the fabric. A bias edge is easier to turn under (hand appliqué) and will fray less than one on the straight of grain.

3. Trace around the template. The sandpaper board will hold the fabric in place while you trace. Make a line you can see! Be sure to draw the line right up next to the edge of the template. It won't matter if the line is wide. It gets turned under in hand appliqué and is cut off in casual appliqué and fusible appliqué.

Trace onto fabric for hand appliqué.

Trace onto paper backing for fusible appliqué.

Place templates with as many edges as possible on bias.

4. For **hand appliqué,** cut out each appliqué piece, adding a ³⁄₁₆˝ turn-under allowance. Add a scant ³⁄₈˝ allowance to any part of an appliqué piece that lies under another piece.

For **fusible appliqué,** cut out each appliqué piece on the drawn line. Add a scant ¹⁄₁₆˝ allowance to any part of an appliqué piece that lies under another piece. Do not remove the paper backing from the fusible appliqué pieces until you are ready to position each piece on the block.

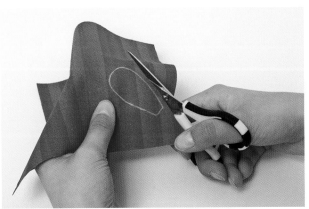

Hand appliqué

Fusible appliqué

Cut out each appliqué piece.

MAKING THE POSITIONING OVERLAY

The positioning overlay is a piece of clear vinyl (page 8) that is used to position each appliqué piece accurately on the block. The overlay is easy to make and use, and it makes your projects portable. It can be used with just about any appliqué method.

1. Cut a piece of the vinyl to the finished size of each block. If your vinyl has a tissue paper lining, cut the vinyl and tissue at the same time and set aside the tissue paper until you are ready to fold or store the overlay. If your vinyl isn't wide enough, you can tape 2 pieces together with clear tape, front and back.

2. Copy the patterns in this book as indicated. Tape together the copies as needed.

❖ MAKING BIG COPIES

Copiers that make very large copies are becoming much more common. Be sure to check with your local copy services to see if they can copy these patterns in one step onto large paper.

3. Tape the pattern onto a table to keep it from shifting.

4. Tape the vinyl over the pattern. Use a ruler and a Sharpie Ultra Fine Point Permanent Marker to draw the pattern's horizontal and vertical center lines onto the vinyl.

5. Accurately trace all the lines from the pattern onto the vinyl. The numbers on the pattern indicate the stitching sequence—include these numbers on the overlay. They also tell you which side of the overlay is the right side.

Tape vinyl over pattern, and draw center lines, pattern lines, and numbers.

6. Draw a small X in one corner of the positioning overlay.

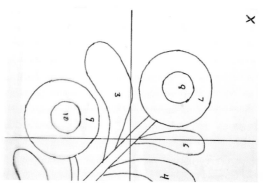

Draw small X in one corner of overlay.

7. To store the overlay, place the tissue paper over the drawn side of the overlay, and fold or roll them together.

USING THE POSITIONING OVERLAY

1. Place the background right side up on the work surface. For hand appliqué, we like to work on top of our sandpaper board. The sandpaper will keep the background from shifting as you position appliqué pieces on the block. For fusible appliqué, work on your ironing surface.

2. Place the overlay right side up on top of the background.

3. Line up the pressed-in center lines in your background with the center lines of the overlay.

♣ TIP

The first time you use the overlay for a block, mark an X on the block in the same corner as on the overlay so that you always know how to position the overlay.

4. Pin the overlay if necessary to keep it from shifting out of position. Flat flower-head pins work best.

Place overlay on background, and line up center lines.

5. For **hand appliqué,** finger-press the turn-under allowances before placing the appliqué pieces on the block. This is not necessary for fusible appliqué but is a very important step for hand appliqué. As you finger-press, make sure that the drawn line is pressed to the back. This one step makes needle-turning the turn-under allowance much easier.

♣ FINGER-PRESSING

Finger-pressing is a very important step in needle-turn hand appliqué. You'll be amazed at how much easier this one step makes needle-turning the turn-under allowance.

Hold the appliqué piece right side up. Use your thumb and index finger to turn the turn-under allowance to the back of the appliqué so that the chalk line is just barely turned under. If you can see the chalk line on the top of your appliqué, it will be visible after it is sewn.

Use your fingers to press a crease into the fabric along the inside of the chalk line. Good-quality 100% cotton will hold a finger-press very well. Do not wet your fingers or use starch or scrape your fingernail along the crease. Just pinch it with your fingertips. Finger-press every edge that will be sewn down. As you are sewing, the fabric will turn on the crease.

Finger-press each piece with drawn line to back.

6. For **fusible appliqué**, peel off the paper backing from each appliqué piece as you go. Be careful not to stretch or ravel the outer edges.

7. Place the appliqué pieces right side up under the overlay but on top of the background. It is easy to tell when the appliqué pieces are in position under the overlay. Start with the #1 appliqué piece, and be sure to place the appliqué pieces in numerical order. Position one piece at a time.

For **hand appliqué**, fold the overlay back, and pin the appliqué pieces in place. You can pin against the sandpaper board; doing so does not dull pins. We usually position and stitch only 1 or 2 pieces at a time. Remove the vinyl overlay before stitching.

For **fusible appliqué**, you may be able to position several pieces at once.

Hand appliqué: Use overlay to position appliqué pieces.

Fusible appliqué: Use overlay to position appliqué pieces

8. Use ½˝ sequin pins, and place pins parallel to (and ¼˝ inside of) the chalk line. It is often easier to baste large pieces to your background. Baste securely parallel to (and ¼˝ inside of) the chalk line.

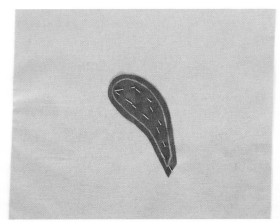

Hand appliqué and pin appliqué pieces in place.

9. For **hand appliqué**, sew the pieces in place with an invisible stitch and matching thread by hand.

For **fusible appliqué**, carefully remove the overlay, and iron the appliqué pieces in place. Be sure to follow the manufacturer's instructions for your brand of fusible web. Do not touch the overlay vinyl with the iron, because the vinyl will melt. After fusing cotton fabric, we recommend that you stitch around the outside of all the fused pieces either by hand or machine. A blanket stitch in matching thread will lend a more traditional feel on these solid fabrics. As the quilts are used, the stitching keeps the edges secure.

10. When you are ready to put away the overlay, place the saved tissue paper over the drawn side before you fold it. The tissue paper will keep the lines from transferring from one part of the vinyl to another.

♣ FOR YOUR INFORMATION

We don't trim the fabric behind our appliqué. We believe that leaving the background intact makes the quilt stronger. And should the quilt ever need to be repaired, it's easier if the background has not been cut.

PRESSING AND TRIMMING THE BLOCKS

After the appliqué is complete, press the blocks on the wrong side. If the ironing surface is hard, place the blocks on a towel so the appliqué will not get flattened. Be careful not to stretch the blocks as you press. Take your time when trimming your blocks to size. Be sure of your measurements *before* you cut. If you are using a ruler, remember to measure twice, and cut once.

❖ TRIMMING TIPS

Always look carefully at your block before you trim. We add 1″ to each side of the finished size when we cut the background for each block and border. You should be trimming off about ¾″ from each edge of your block. If you are about to trim much more (or less) than that, check your measurements.

Use the short lines that you drew over the ends of the pressed-in grid to help you center your cuts.

Take your time. If it helps you visualize how much you need to trim away, compare your paper pattern to your block.

1. Press the blocks on the wrong side.

2. Carefully trim each block to size. Refer to the ¼″ lines you drew in the center of each of the 4 edges of your backgrounds to help you center your blocks.

Special Appliqué Techniques

CUTAWAY APPLIQUÉ

The cutaway technique makes it much easier to stitch irregular, long, thin, or very small pieces. It is especially good to use for narrow stems like those in *All Wonderful Red & Green.*

1. Place the template on top of the selected fabric. Be sure to place the template on the fabric so that most of the edges will be on the diagonal grain of the fabric. Trace around the template.

Place template with as many edges as possible on bias, and trace around template.

2. Cut out the appliqué piece, leaving ¾˝ or more of excess fabric around the traced shape. Leave fabric intact in the V between points, inside deep curves, and so on.

3. Finger-press, making sure the drawn line is pressed to the back.

4. Use the vinyl positioning overlay to position the appliqué piece on the block.

5. Pin the shape in place, keeping pins ¼˝ away from the finger-pressed edge. Place pins parallel to the edges. Large pieces can be basted in place if you prefer. If you baste, pin the shape in place, and then baste it. When a shape is curved, sew the concave side first if possible.

When shapes are narrow, one row of pins may be sufficient. In this case, place pins ¼˝ away from the edge you will sew first.

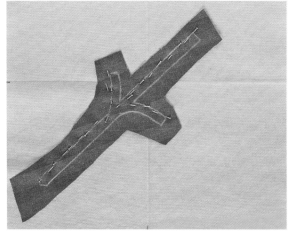

Pin appliqué piece in place; baste large shapes.

6. Begin trimming the excess fabric away from where you will start stitching, leaving a ³⁄₁₆˝ turn-under allowance. Never start stitching at an inner or outer point that will be turned and stitched under.

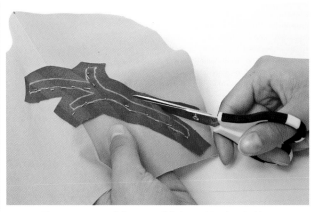

Cut away some of the excess fabric, and begin stitching.

7. Trim more fabric as you sew. Clip inner curves and inner points as needed.

8. Remove the pins as you stitch the next side of the piece. Trim excess fabric as necessary.

9. Continue until all sides of the appliqué piece are stitched.

✿ TIP

Appliquéing the doors and windows of houses: The door and the door's trim are best sewn together before appliquéing the unit to the block. Leave the door fabric bigger because it's easier to hold on to. Trace the door trim template onto the trim fabric. Use the cutaway appliqué technique to sew the trim to the door fabric. Use the door template to cut the door and trim together, leaving 3⁄16″ seam allowance. Sew the unit in place.

Windows are handled the same way, except that you cut out the center of the window trim fabric to sew it to the window fabric.

CIRCLE APPLIQUÉ

When sewing outer curves and circles, you can only control one stitch at a time. Use the needle or a round wooden toothpick to smooth out any pleats that form. Remember, the more you practice, the better you'll get.

1. Prepare and position the circles as you would any other appliqué piece, including finger-pressing each circle. If you are pinning rather than basting, use 2 or more pins to hold the circle in place. Never use just 1 pin, as the circle can shift out of place as you sew.

2. Begin sewing. Turn under only enough turn-under allowance to take 1 or 2 stitches. If you turn under more than that, the edge will either flatten or a pleat will form, causing a point.

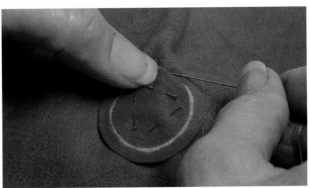

Turn under only enough for 1 or 2 stitches.

3. If a pleat forms, use the tip of the needle or toothpick to reach under the appliqué to spread open the fold. The point will smooth out as you open up the pleat.

4. To close the circle, turn under the last few stitches all at once. The circle will tend to flatten out.

5. Use the tip of the needle to smooth out the pleats in the turn-under allowance and to pull the flattened part of the circle into a more rounded shape.

ABOUT THE AUTHORS

They started Piece O' Cake Designs in 1994, as they were each moving away from Tulsa. Becky and her husband headed for Sherman, Texas, with their two sons. Linda and her husband, Paul, moved first to Pagosa Springs, Colorado, back to Tulsa in 2001, and finally to Grand Junction, Colorado in 2008.

Linda owned and managed a beauty salon before she started quilting. Over the years she developed a fine eye for color as a hair colorist and makeup artist. Becky's degree is in interior design with a liberal sprinkling of art classes. They think that their varied backgrounds have combined well, making the quilts they design distinctive.

Becky and Linda initially self-published their patterns and books but are now very happy members of the C&T Publishing family.

Visit Becky and Linda at their website www.pieceocake.com and their blog at http://pieceocakeblog.blogspot.com.

Becky and Linda first met at the Green Country Quilter's Guild in Tulsa, Oklahoma, where they both held up their hands and volunteered for jobs at their very first guild meetings. As they worked together on many guild projects, their friendship grew through a shared love for quilting, and for appliqué in particular.

Also by Becky Goldsmith and Linda Jenkins:

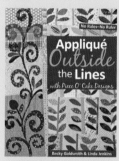

Also available as an eBook

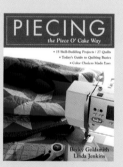

Also available as an eBook

Also available as an eBook

Also available as a POD book

Also available as an eBook

Also available as an eBook

SOURCES

Look for Shape-Flex All-Purpose Woven Fusible Interfacing at your local quilt shop, or order it online from C&T Publishing.

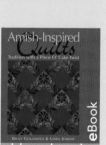

Great Titles *from* C&T PUBLISHING & STASH BOOKS

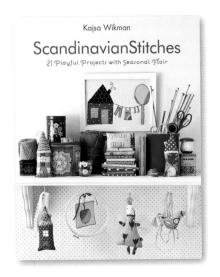

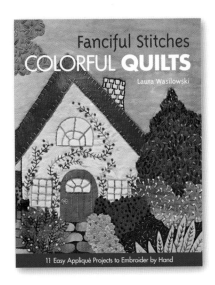

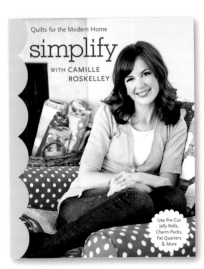

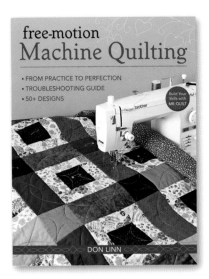

Available at your local retailer or **www.ctpub.com** *or* **800-284-1114**

For a list of other fine books from C&T Publishing, visit our website
to view our catalog online.

C&T PUBLISHING, INC.

P.O. Box 1456
Lafayette, CA 94549
800-284-1114

Email: ctinfo@ctpub.com
Website: www.ctpub.com

C&T Publishing's professional photography services are now available to
the public. Visit us at www.ctmediaservices.com.

Tips and Techniques can be found at www.ctpub.com > Consumer
Resources > Quiltmaking Basics: Tips & Techniques for Quiltmaking & More

For quilting supplies:

COTTON PATCH

1025 Brown Ave.
Lafayette, CA 94549
Store: 925-284-1177
Mail order: 925-283-7883

Email: CottonPa@aol.com
Website: www.quiltusa.com

Note: Fabrics used in the quilts shown may not be currently
available, as fabric manufacturers keep most fabrics in print for
only a short time.